HUMOROUS MONOLOGUES

BY MARTHA BOLTON

PICTURES BY JOYCE Behr
FOREWORD BY BOB HOPE

Sterling Publishing Co., Inc.   New York

Library of Congress Cataloging-in-Publication Data

Bolton, Martha.
    Humorous monologues / by Martha Bolton ; illustrations by Joyce
Behr ; foreword by Bob Hope.
      p. cm.
    Includes index.
    Summary: Presents a collection of humorous monologues divided
into such categories as historical, holiday, and fairy tale and nursery
rhyme spoofs.
    ISBN 0-8069-6750-1
    1. Monologues. 2. Acting—Juvenile literature. [1. Monologues.
2. Acting.] I. Behr, Joyce, ill. II. Title.
PN2080.B6 1989
812′.54—dc19   88-25977
                                                    CIP
                                                    AC

Copyright © 1989 by Martha Bolton
Published by Sterling Publishing Co., Inc.
Two Park Avenue, New York, N.Y. 10016
Distributed in Canada by Oak Tree Press Ltd.
℅ Canadian Manda Group, P.O. Box 920, Station U
Toronto, Ontario, Canada M8Z 5P9
Distributed in Great Britain and Europe by Cassell PLC
Artillery House, Artillery Row, London SW1P 1RT, England
Distributed in Australia by Capricorn Ltd.
P.O. Box 665, Lane Cove, NSW 2066
Manufactured in the United States of America

To
Gene Perret
and
Robert L. Mills
. . . for so much

Contents

Foreword

I love the sound of laughter. It's the reason why I get up in the morning. I have an alarm clock that doesn't ring; it chuckles. I once cut short a fishing trip when I found out that trout can't laugh.

I've chased the sound of laughter around the world. I've entertained in just about every place on the map, and a few places that don't even show up on most maps. I got a call from some soldiers on a remote island in the Indian Ocean once. When I agreed to bring our troupe there for a visit, they asked, "How long do you think it will take you to fly here?" I said, "I don't know. Why?" They said, "We have to know how much time we have to build a landing strip."

They not only made a great runway, but they also made a great audience.

That's the great thing about laughter, too. It sounds exactly the same coming from soldiers sitting on the grass in an open-air arena as it does from the King and Queen sitting in the Royal Box.

It's a happy sound. It's the sound of people having fun. I can guarantee from a lifetime of experience that the person hearing the laughs has as much fun as the people doing the laughing.

That's why this book of Martha Bolton's is

so priceless. It's going to introduce the art of the humorous monologue to a lot of people, and it's going to acquaint a lot of people with the fun of doing comedy.

What a thrill you're in for when you hear your first laughs. I don't even remember the first joke I ever told. I don't know if that's because my memory is bad, or the joke was. But I do remember the laughs.

Humor is enjoying a tremendous rebirth right now. There are comedy stores opening up in every city in the nation, and the comics who are graduating from them are good. I see many of the young comedians and they're funny. They're so funny, it scares me. It makes me go home and throw more coals on my writers.

It's a good sign that we're laughing more and enjoying it more. Humor is healthy. And a nation that can laugh at itself, like we do, is a strong, free, vibrant nation.

I travel around this country often and I always carry a satchel full of ad-libs with me— a briefcase full of "goodies" that my writers have prepared as a bon-voyage gift for me.

You've got the same thing, now, neatly bound and contained between the covers of this book. There's some good, funny, hip material here on many different topics. Have fun with it.

Of course, the secret behind any good comedian is the writer. You've got a fine one in this collection of monologues—Martha Bolton. Just remember, though, she's *my* writer. I only lent her to you folks long enough to write this book. I need her back. You never know when someone may ask me to say something funny.

Martha knows funny. She's been writing it for different people in different fields for several years now. First of all, she's been an award-winning newspaper columnist. She's written gag-lines for top cartoonists. She's got a whole series of best-sellers in the bookstores. And she also writes for me—I guess, in her spare time.

In this book, you've got a writer who certainly has the credentials and you've got a nice selection of funny material to choose from. All you need now is a little rehearsal time, an audience, and you're off to your comedy career.

Use this book well and be merciless—get as many laughs as you can from your listeners. But do me a favor, will you—leave a few laughs for us old-timers too, huh?

Thanks.

Bob Hope
February, 1988

Before You Begin

I still remember the very first school play I was in. It was called *The Land of the Incas*, and I played a puma.

On cue I was to race across the stage on all fours, making the kind of noise a puma makes. I didn't quite know what that was, but my teacher assured me it was similar to the noises I enjoyed making in class anyway.

And besides, getting me down on all fours was the only way to balance out the height difference between me and the other students. You see, I was tall for my age—too tall to ever play the romantic leads. When I tried out for the role of Pocahontas, I got the totem pole part instead. And I didn't get picked to play Juliet because they were afraid when they added my height to the height of the balcony, the only way Romeo and I could communicate would be to yodel.

But the puma role seemed tailor-made for me, and even though my performance may have only brought to mind the first part of my character (the P.U.), it was fun.

And that's how it should be. Whether you forget a line, miss a cue, or the sound effects don't quite come in where they're supposed to, the bottom line is to have fun.

That's what this book is all about.

Performance Tips

The monologues in this book were written to be performed in front of a live audience. A live audience is recommended because the other kind rarely applauds.

The set and prop requirements have been kept to a minimum, and costumes may be as elaborate or as simple as your budget allows.

Depending upon the desire of the director, scripts may either by memorized or read.

For easy reference, the monologues have been divided into five categories: Fairy Tale Spoofs, Nursery Rhyme Spoofs, Holiday, Historical, and Grab Bag.

Covering everything from Columbus discovering America to Little Bo Peep filing a "missing sheep" report with the police, these monologues are ideal for class programs, PTA talent shows, school assemblies, or any other fun event.

In fact, you may want to use them just to entertain your own family. But remember, if it's an after-dinner show, clear the plates first. Why give the critics ammunition?

NURSERY
RHYME
SPOOFS

"I kept telling him, 'Use a stuntman!
Use a stuntman!'"

The Life and Times of Humpty Dumpty

CHARACTER: News reporter (boy or girl)
SETTING: A mock brick wall
PROPS: A hand-held microphone
COSTUME: Business attire

(NEWS REPORTER IS STANDING IN FRONT OF THE BRICK WALL, HOLDING THE MICROPHONE AND LOOKING INTO AN IMAGINARY TELEVISION CAMERA.)

Ladies and gentlemen, I am here standing in front of the very wall off which Mr. Dumpty, "Humpty" to his many friends and fans, fell earlier today. This is a most tragic and solemn moment.

Our mini-cams were on the scene within minutes of the accident, and have remained here throughout the day while all the king's horses and all the king's men attempted to put Humpty Dumpty back together again. Let's see if we can talk to one of them now.

(MIMES WORKING HIS WAY THROUGH CROWD) Excuse me, sir, but just how serious does it look for Mr. Dumpty? . . . You say it could go either way? He could fully recover or be Eggs Benedict by morning? Only time will tell? (SIGHS) Well, sir, I want to commend you and the other king's men on all that you've done. I've been watching you guys scrambling around here—no pun intended—making sure everything that can be done is being done. And I even understand some of the nation's top Crazy Glue specialists have been called in and are working around the clock. One thing's for certain, Humpty Dumpty is in the best of hands!

(INTO CAMERA) And so, while we await word of Humpty Dumpty's condition, our station felt this would be a good time for a retrospective of his illustrious and legendary career.

After being discovered in the dairy case of a Hollywood grocery store, Humpty was cast in a supporting role in the film classic "Cheaper By The Dozen." From there he moved on to star in such notable movies as "The Breakfast Club," "The Egg Who Came To Dinner," and what many have termed his finest film, "The Good, The Bad, and The Hard-Boiled."

Humpty was a private person. No matter how hard you tried, you just couldn't seem to get past his outer shell. He was a well-rounded individual, and even though some say he wasn't all he was cracked up to be, he was still considered a "good egg" by those who knew him best.

He never complained when we'd paint him funny colors at Eastertime or toss his relatives around at a July 4th picnic.

Yes, Humpty Dumpty (WIPING A TEAR FROM HIS EYE), you're quite a guy! And wherever you are right now, I hope you know we're all rooting for you! . . . I'd throw in, "and that's no 'yoke' ", but I'm sure in your line of work, you've been around enough hams.

So, let me just close by saying, "Good luck, and always remember to keep your sunny side up!"

This is (FILL IN YOUR NAME) reporting from (FILL IN CITY). Good night.

BLACKOUT

"I said, 'Order bottled water,' but would you listen? No!"

Jack's Big Headache

CHARACTER: Jack (of Jack and Jill fame)
SETTING: Doctor's office
PROPS: A metal pail
COSTUME: Ordinary clothing

(JACK IS PACING ON STAGE. THE PAIL IS "STUCK" ON HIS HEAD. HOWEVER, IT SHOULDN'T COVER HIS MOUTH.)

. . . But, doctor, what do you mean it *won't* come off? It's GOT to come off! You can't expect me to go through life with a bucket stuck on my head. I mean, I've heard of being into heavy metal, but this is ridiculous!

And besides, I could get hurt in here. The last time I sneezed, it ricocheted for fifteen minutes!

Oh, why'd I ever go up that hill with Jill to fetch a pail of water in the first place? I should have just told her to use the drinking fountain like everyone else.

But, noooo! I had to try to *impress* her. I thought she was *cute*. I thought she was *nice*. I thought she was . . . *thirsty*!

And now, after all the trouble I went through for her, she's nowhere in sight! . . . But then, right now *everyone's* nowhere in sight!

So, tell me, doc, can you get it off? Tomorrow is class picture day, and I can't go like this. (TURNS HEAD TO RIGHT, THEN TO LEFT, POSING) How will I know which is my best side?

But, hey, don't get me wrong. I realize there are advantages to my predicament. This could save me a fortune on haircuts. And I could easily get away with sleeping in class, although, my snoring might echo.

But still, this isn't the look for me. I mean, aluminum's nice, but it's definitely not my color.

Say, maybe if we both work at it . . . (HE STARTS PULLING AT THE FRONT OF THE PAIL, BUT IT DOESN'T BUDGE) Okay, this time you pull the front and I'll work at it from the back. (HE PULLS AT THE BACK AND IT BUDGES JUST A LITTLE.) Hey, wait a minute! I think it's coming! (HE STRUGGLES WITH IT SOME MORE.) Yes! Yes! I can feel something loosening. It's either the pail . . . or my head!

(HE CONTINUES PULLING AT THE PAIL.) That's it! That's it! It's coming! (HE STRUGGLES WITH IT SOME MORE, GRITTING HIS TEETH IN SHEER DETERMINATION. SUDDENLY, THE

PAIL POPS OFF.) Whew! (HOLDING THE BUCKET IN HIS HAND, HE RUBS HIS HEAD.) That was a close one!

And trust me, doc, I've learned my lesson. The next time a girl asks me to fetch a pail of water, her notebook had better be on fire!

(HE TURNS AND STARTS TO EXIT.) Well, see you, doc. And thanks! (HE MIMES OPENING A DOOR, THEN STOPS SUDDENLY AND TURNS BACK.)

Boy, I tell you, doc, today just isn't your day. Now there's a guy in your waiting room who's got his thumb stuck in a pie! . . . I wonder who he was trying to impress—Sara Lee? (HE SHRUGS HIS SHOULDERS AND EXITS WITH PAIL IN HAND.)

BLACKOUT

"All right, guys, if we want to live, this is how it's got to be. As soon as he starts to huff and puff, I'll open the door, and you spray the breath freshener!"

Pig, Pig, and Pig vs. The Big Bad Wolf

CHARACTER:	Attorney for The Big Bad Wolf
SETTING:	Courtroom
PROPS:	None needed
COSTUME:	Business suit
SPECIAL EFFECTS:	A fan (offstage, preferably operated by adults—it makes them feel important. But keep an eye on them, so that they don't hurt themselves.)

(ATTORNEY IS PACING BACK AND FORTH.)

Ladies and gentlemen of the jury, you have heard the testimony of these two, uh, pardon the expression, "pigs." They have stated that my client, The Big Bad Wolf, huffed and puffed and blew their houses in.

Now, I'll admit my client's breath could melt dental equipment, but knock over a house? I doubt it.

And, anyway, how do they know it was my client huffing and puffing on their porches? Who's to say it wasn't an out-of-shape Avon lady?

And then there's the question of motive. *Why* would my client want to blow their houses down in the first place? To put up condominiums?

No, ladies and gentlemen, I submit to you that my client, Mr. Wolf, is totally innocent of these charges. And furthermore, he is an upstanding member of the community. Okay, so he sheds on the furniture at City Hall, and drools when he speaks at PTA meetings; but, hey, none of us are perfect!

And now, let's consider the testimony of the third pig. He has stated that after Pigs #1 and #2 ran to his brick home for safety, my client tried to blow his house down as well. Then, when he failed to do so, he attempted illegal entry through the chimney with the full intentions of eating all three little pigs.

(LAUGHS) Why, that's the most preposterous thing I've ever heard! My client is on a pork-free diet. For him it's Wolf-Chow or nothing!

Therefore, ladies and gentlemen of the

jury, I know that when you consider all the evidence which has been presented today, you'll know there's only one question to ask and only one answer to give. Is my client guilty? Not by a hair on his chinney chin chin!

But alas, maybe he should answer for himself. (TURNS AND LOOKS OFFSTAGE) Mr. Wolf, do you have anything you'd like to say? (AT THIS POINT, YOUR ASSISTANT TURNS ON THE OFFSTAGE FAN. THE ATTORNEY IS HIT WITH A BLAST OF WIND, STRUGGLES TO STAY UPRIGHT, BUT SEEMS LIKELY TO BE BLOWN AWAY AT ANY MOMENT. TURNING TO AUDIENCE)

On second thought, perhaps we should just plead guilty!

BLACKOUT

"I had a feeling I should have taken the elevator!"

Because It's There

CHARACTER: Eency Weency Spider

SETTING: In front of a giant water spout

PROPS: Several buckets of water (optional—you can mime this action if desired. But if you use real water place a plastic canvas on the floor to protect it.)

COSTUME: Spider costume

(EENCY WEENCY IS STANDING BY THE WATER SPOUT, QUITE FRUSTRATED.)

One more time. I'm gonna climb up this water spout one more time, and if the rain comes down and washes me out again, this eency weency spider's out of here!

I mean, how does it look? An insect of my reputation and community standing watersliding down drain pipes? Why, the last spider they caught doing that is now sporting an eight-armed straitjacket down at Bellevue!

Actually, I don't really know why I want to climb up there anyway. It's not for the view. I mean, let's face it, this place will *never* make the cover of *Better Webs and Gardens*. And it's not for the exercise. I get enough of a workout doing my daily jumping jacks. . . . 'Course every third jumping jack, I've got to stop and untangle my arms!

No . . . (PACING) I guess I'd have to say I want to climb up this waterspout for the mere challenge of it. You know— (DRAMATIC) because it's there!

(LOOKING UP) And now that the sun has returned again, I'll give it just one more try. (MIMES CLIMBING) You see, I *know* I'm going to make it up this ol' waterspout someday. (CLIMBS SOME MORE) All I need is a little perseverance, (CONTINUES TO CLIMB) a little determination (CLIMBS SOME MORE) and . . . (A BUCKET OF WATER POURS DOWN FROM THE TOP OF THE WATERSPOUT. THE BUCKET, THOUGH, SHOULD NOT BE SEEN BY THE AUDIENCE. EENCY MIMES BEING WASHED DOWN THE SPOUT BY THE WATER. NOW, QUITE DRENCHED, LOOKING UP TOWARD THE TOP OF THE SPOUT) . . . and a lot more dependable weather reports!

(SLOWLY, GETTING UP AND WRINGING SELF OUT) But, is Eency Weency a quitter? *No!* (LOOKS UP) And now since the sun has graciously returned to the sky again, this spider's making the big move! (MIMES CLIMBING UP THE WATERSPOUT ONCE MORE) This spider's climbing upward to victory! (CONTINUES CLIMBING) This spider's reaching for new heights, and not looking back! (ANOTHER BUCKET OF WATER POURS DOWN. HE FROWNS AMIDST THE SHOWER) This spider's gotta move to a drier climate!

(DETERMINED) All right, this is it! (SHAKES DRY) No more Mr. Nice Guy! This time I'm really going to do it! This time I'm going all the way to the top! (STANDING TALL AND CONFIDENT) This time there'll be no stopping me!

This time . . . I'm taking the elevator! (TURNS AND EXITS, TRIUMPHANTLY)

BLACKOUT

"I hoped it wouldn't come to this."

Sheep Gone Bad

CHARACTER: Little Bo-Peep

SETTING: Police Station—Mother Gooseland Precinct

PROPS: Free-standing reception counter
Shepherd's staff
Mug sketch of the Big Bad Wolf, side and front views (sketch should be lying down on the counter)

COSTUME: Bo-Peep attire (available at your finer Bo-Peep Dress Shops)

(BO-PEEP RUSHES INTO POLICE STATION IN A PANIC, TRUSTY SHEPHERD'S CROOK IN HAND.)

Officer, officer, you've got to help me! I'm Little Bo-Peep and I've lost my sheep! . . . You say you're Officer Blair and you've lost your hair? (UNAMUSED) Sir, this is serious. I need you to put out an all-points bulletin on my sheep right away!

. . . What do you mean they have to be missing for twenty-four hours?! Why, do you realize what all can happen to them in twenty-four hours? (PACING) They could get mugged! They could get assaulted! They could get sheepnapped and sheared against their will! . . . Now, mind you, I'm not one to panic, but I *did* see a Ferrari sporting some sheepskin seatcovers that looked an awful lot like . . . well, I just don't want to think about it!

(GLANCES DOWN ON THE COUNTER AND GASPS) And don't tell me *he's* still out there! (SHE LIFTS UP THE MUG SHOT OF THE BIG BAD WOLF SO THE AUDIENCE CAN SEE IT) . . . Mutton Enemy Number One! The Ol' Lamb Chop Bandit himself! The Big Bad Wolf! . . . Now I *know* we've got to move fast!

(SETS THE MUG SHOT DOWN AND STARTS TO PACE AGAIN) . . . And there's another thing to consider. Out there on the streets, it's hard to stay an innocent lamb for long. What if they fall in with the wrong flock? You know, start hanging out in sleazy pastures with evil and corrupt sheep—sheep who are running from the law. Sheep taking it on the lam, so to speak. (BUILDING) Then, finding themselves hungry and cold, they, too, will turn to a life of crime. But sooner or later you'll catch up to them. You'll slap the hoof-cuffs on them and haul them off to jail. Why?

(SHOUTING AND STOMPING HER FEET) *Because you had to wait the twenty-four hours before going to look for them in the first place!!*

(CALMLY) Now, do we fill out that "Missing Sheep" form or not? (SMILES TRIUMPHANTLY) Good. . . . You say you'll need to know what they were wearing when I last saw them? . . . Why, wool, of course. . . . I know it's too hot for wool, but polyester gives them a rash.

Oh, and here's another tip. They always travel together. They figure they can split the cab fare that way!

. . . Now, I suppose the best thing for me to do is to go back home and. . . . (TURNS TO EXIT BUT STOPS SUDDENLY AS IF SHE JUST SAW SOMETHING OUT THE WINDOW) . . . Wait a minute! *There* they are! They're over there across the street . . . at the video arcade! . . . Umpf! I might have known! (STARTS TO LEAVE, THEN TURNS BACK) Boy, I tell ya, Mary doesn't know how good she's got it. She only has one lamb to look after!

(AS SHE EXITS, SHE YELLS OFFSTAGE AS IF TO SHEEP.) All right, that's it! You're all grounded!

BLACKOUT

"And it even has a sunken living room—thanks to that last earthquake."

What a Bargain!

CHARACTER: Real estate salesman

SETTING: On the sidewalk in front of the house that Jack built (The house need not be part of the set.)

PROPS: Briefcase, with papers inside

COSTUME: A business suit

(THE SALESMAN, BRIEFCASE IN HAND, IS ENTHUSIASTICALLY SHOWING OFF THE PROPERTY)

I'm telling you, you won't find a better bargain on the real estate market today! This house that Jack built is sturdy, solid, and it's been totally refurbished.

What's that? (LEANS TOWARD IMAGINARY CUSTOMER TO HEAR, THEN LOOKS OFF TO THE SIDE) Oh, that's nothing. That's just some malt that lay in the house that Jack built. Someone must have spilt it.

Now, getting back to the business at hand. (OPENS BRIEFCASE AND TAKES

OUT SOME PAPERS) You'll be happy to know that this house comes with . . . What's that? (LEANS IN AGAIN TO LISTEN) A rat? (LOOKS AROUND) I don't see any rats. (THEN SUDDENLY NOTICING SOMETHING OFF TO THE LEFT) Oh, *that* rat. That's just the rat that ate the malt that lay in the house that Jack built.

(ASIDE TO SOMEONE OFFSTAGE) Quick! Get a cat in here! You think I can sell a house with rats in it?!

(TURNING BACK TO IMAGINARY CUSTOMER) Now then, where were we? I believe I was just about to tell you some of the features of this . . . (LOOKS DOWN) Ah, here we go. Here's the cat that killed that rat that ate the malt that lay in the house that Jack built.

So, now that that's taken care of, shall we talk finances? (LEANS FORWARD AGAIN) Excuse me? What barking? (LISTENING FOR A MOMENT) Oh, that? That's the dog that worried the cat that killed the rat that ate the malt that lay in the house that Jack built.

Now then, what sort of down payment were you prepared to put toward this beautiful, custom home?

What cow? (LOOKS AROUND) Oh, *that* cow. The one with the crumpled horn. I *told* him to quit using it for a can-opener, but would he listen? No!

So, now that you've seen the cow with the crumpled horn that tossed the dog that worried the cat that killed the rat that ate the malt that lay in the house that Jack built, what do you have to say? Is it a deal or what?

. . . What's that? You say you'd like to look at a few more homes?

. . . Well, my friend, this is your lucky day! Why, three very lovely homes came on the market just this morning. Some pigs used to live in them, but they did have great decorating tastes. . . . 'Tho, to be perfectly honest, I think the brick one's a bit overpriced. Still, I can probably get you a good deal on the other two. (LEADING CUSTOMER OFFSTAGE AND CONTINUING THE HARD SELL) Sure, they're a little windblown, but, hey, with some paint, some paneling, some framework, some roofing, some plumbing. . . .

BLACKOUT

"I wouldn't mind her following me to school every day, but does she have to get better grades than me?"

Who's the New Kid with the Hoofs?
(or)
Mary Had a Little Problem

CHARACTER: Mary (of "Had a Little Lamb" fame)

SETTING: On the road to school

PROPS: School books

COSTUME: Dress, shoes and socks

(MARY, BOOKS IN HAND, ENTERS SKIPPING. SHE TURNS TO LOOK BEHIND HER, THEN STOPS AND SHAKES HER HEAD IN FRUSTRATION. SHE THEN SPEAKS TO HER LAMB WHO IS, OF COURSE, UNSEEN BY THE AUDIENCE.)

Go on! Get! How many times do I have to tell you, you *can't* come to school with me!

You're a lamb! And I don't think lambs are considered foreign exchange students!

So, c'mon! Take off my school sweater and put my bookbag back where you found it. It was a nice try, but Mr. Sternly, the school principal, would never let an animal onto the campus. Okay, sure, there *are* a few sixth graders he considers animals, but at least they don't eat the soccer field.

Now, go on. (COAXING) Go on. (SHE BREATHES A SIGH OF RELIEF, SKIPS A FEW STEPS, THEN STOPS AND LOOKS TO HER SIDE.) No, no, I meant go *that* way. (SHE POINTS IN THE OPPOSITE DIRECTION.)

Aw, look, even if you *did* make it past Mr. Sternly, you don't think you could fool my teacher, Miss Trebble, do you? She'd notice you sooner or later . . . like when you started going "baa" in class, or nibbling on our fungus experiments. After all, she didn't let me get away with that, why should she let you?

And don't think they're going to serve you grass in the cafeteria. This is Monday. That's Thursday's main course.

So, go now. Get going. (ONCE AGAIN COAXING) There. That's a good girl. (TO AUDIENCE) Hey, it's nothing against her personally. It's just that school's no place for a lamb. I mean, why would a lamb need to learn arithmetic? Unless, of course, she can't get to sleep and has to start counting people. And why should a lamb bother learning cursive writing? Isn't printing good enough? Then, there's peer pressure to consider. Everyone knows sheep just follow the crowd.

No, she's much better off back at home, and she knows it. That's why she finally agreed to. . . . (LOOKS AT HER SIDE, THEN SHAKES HER HEAD) What are *you* still doing here?! (TO AUDIENCE) Oh, well, what else should I expect from an Obedience School drop-out?

(PLEADING TO LAMB) C'mon, you've got to get going before someone sees you with me. There *is* that new leash law, you know. You want me to get fined?

Now, go on. Be a good girl. (THREATENING) Or do I finally get that new wool coat I've been wanting? (SMILES TRIUMPHANTLY) Aha! I thought that might persuade you. (BRIEF PAUSE, THEN CUPPING HER HANDS, SHE YELLS.) And don't forget to wait for the crossing guard!

(SHE GIVES A DEEP SIGH, THEN LOOKS OUT TOWARD THE AUDIENCE.) Whew! That was a close one! (SHE STARTS TO CONTINUE SKIPPING TOWARD SCHOOL, THEN STOPS SUDDENLY. SHE

TURNS TO THE AUDIENCE.) Oh, but don't get me wrong. I love her. But I just hope she outgrows this before I go to college! (SHE SHAKES HER HEAD, THEN SKIPS OFFSTAGE.)

BLACKOUT

FAIRY TALE SPOOFS

"Don't worry, son. If they ate your mother's cooking, they couldn't have gotten far."

Goldilocks's Day in Court

CHARACTER:	Goldilocks
SETTING:	Courtroom
PROPS:	Witness chair
COSTUME:	A dress, shoes and socks
	Gold curls

(GOLDILOCKS IS SITTING IN THE WITNESS CHAIR. SHE TURNS TOWARD IMAGINARY JUDGE.)

But, your honor, I've already told you everything that happened that day.

I was just walking through the forest—it's a short-cut to the 7-11 store—and I came upon this cute little cottage.

The door was open, so I just peeked in and saw three bowls of porridge on the table. Frankly, I was hoping for lobster and Perrier, but this is a low-budget fairy tale.

Now, the first bowl of porridge was way too salty. The second bowl was far too sweet. And the third bowl was just as lousy, which could be why you don't see many fast food porridge restaurants around! But I ate it anyway.

And, yes, I confess I later sat down on one of their chairs and broke it. But you try eating a bowl of that cement mix and see how lightly you sit in your seat!

Then, I was feeling a little woozy from the porridge, and a little sore from the chair incident, so I decided to go upstairs to take a little nap.

I picked the smallest of their three beds to sleep in because it was most like my own— unmade. So, I climbed in and fell fast asleep.

And the next thing I know I've got bear breath beating down on me! I open my eyes and there's Papa Bear, Mama Bear, and Baby Bear, and they're all looking at me like I'm an Alpo chewstick with curls!

. . . And, well, the rest is in the police report.

But you've *got* to believe me, sir. I didn't mean any harm!

. . . Well, yes, I suppose what I did *could* be considered trespassing.

. . . And, yes, I realize I should be held responsible for any damage done to the Bear Family's property.

But, sir, a five hundred dollar fine?! That's pretty steep. Why, on my allowance that'll take me (FIGURING IT OUT ON HER FINGERS) . . . forever!

. . . So, that's it, huh? Five hundred

dollars! I can't plea bargain? I can't throw myself on the mercy of the court? I can't remind you that I *did*, in fact, eat the porridge, and some judges might consider that punishment enough?

(THROWS HANDS UP IN EXASPERATION. OBVIOUSLY, THE JUDGE ISN'T BUDGING.) All right, all right, I'll pay the fine.

(REMORSEFUL) . . . And, yes, your honor, I can honestly say I have learned my lesson. The next time I wander carelessly into someone else's home (DOUBLES OVER AND HOLDS STOMACH) . . . it's going to be someone who can cook! (SHE EXITS, MOANING.)

BLACKOUT

Big Foot and the Prince

CHARACTER:	Cinderella
SETTING:	The intersection of "FAIRY TALE LANE" and "PRINCE BOULEVARD"
PROPS:	Street sign indicating the street names A pumpkin Several rubber mice
COSTUME:	Basic rags. She should be wearing only one shoe, and it should be old and worn out with a slight heel to make her walking uneven.

(CINDERELLA IS LEANING AGAINST THE STREET SIGN. THE PUMPKIN AND MICE ARE DOWN BY HER FEET. SHE IS DISGUSTED.)

This is just great! Here I am, stuck by the side of the road. My beautiful carriage has turned back into a pumpkin, and those magnificent horses are all creepy little mice again. (SHE SIGHS AND SHAKES HER HEAD.) Boy, the Auto Club is *never* gonna believe this one!

(SHE LOOKS DOWN AT HER DRESS AND SNEERS.) And just look at this dress! Five minutes ago it was a lovely ball gown. Now, look at it! I mean, I've heard of being rough on your clothes, but this is ridiculous!

And I still can't believe I ran off and left one of my glass slippers on the palace steps. Let's fact it, most girls just drop a handkerchief. But, nooooo, not me! I've got to drop a size 12, complete with Odor-Eater! You call *that* romantic?

(SIGHS) Still, I *did* get to meet the handsome prince. And, man, oh, man, what a hunk! No wonder his royal poster is the hottest seller in all the land!

And then, when he walked over and asked me to dance . . . (SHE PUTS THE BACK OF HER HAND AGAINST HER FOREHEAD.) . . . why, I just about fainted! You see, before tonight my only dance partners had been brooms and mops, and even they said I had two left feet. Two *big* left feet!

(SIGHS) But, ah, this has been a night to truly remember!

And alas! Now I must start walking home for, obviously, this pumpkin isn't planning on taking me anywhere. It's just as well, though. I hate compact transportation!

(SHE LIMPS A FEW STEPS, THEN STOPS.) And besides, by now the handsome prince has surely found my other shoe, and is, at this very moment, out looking for me!

(SHE SMILES, TAKES OFF HER ONE SHOE, WALKS A FEW STEPS, THEN STOPS. TAKING A WHIFF OF THE SHOE, SHE GRIMACES.)

Either that, or they're still trying to revive him!

BLACKOUT

*"I tell you, that's the last time I'll use
a discount computer dating service!"*

My Love Is Like a Green, Green Frog

CHARACTER: Princess
SETTING: Romantic garden setting
PROPS: None needed
COSTUME: Princess attire

(THE BEAUTIFUL PRINCESS IS STANDING CENTER STAGE. SHE PRETENDS TO HOLD A FROG IN HER HAND, AND IS CONTEMPLATING KISSING IT. THAT'S RIGHT, SHE'S CONTEMPLATING *KISSING* IT!)

Okay, Frog. My fairy godmother told me if I kissed you, you'd turn into a handsome prince. So, tell me, green cheeks, what will a handshake get me? A royal nerd?

(SHE SHAKES HIS HAND, THEN WAITS A FEW MOMENTS.) Ummm, nothing, huh?

But, hey, look, don't get me wrong. It's not that I don't *want* to kiss you. It's just that, . . . well, to be perfectly honest, it's your breath. (SHE HOLDS THE FROG AT ARM'S LENGTH.) Wowee! What'd you have for dinner? Dragonflies in garlic sauce?

And speaking of food . . . (SHE LOOKS HIM OVER.) I see your tongue's been working overtime. C'mon! Suck in that potbelly! . . . And listen, Webfoot, take my advice and lay off those honeybees. Why, do you realize how many calories are in one of those babies?

(SHE ADJUSTS THE FROG A LITTLE.) And for goodness sakes, stand up straight! Who do you think you are? The Hunchback of the Lily Pad?

And tell me, do you ALWAYS have to make that little "noise" of yours? That croaking goes right THROUGH me!

(SHE PAUSES A MOMENT AND SIGHS.) But other than all that, I guess I wouldn't mind kissing you. After all, you ARE better looking than my last blind date!

(SHE TAKES A DEEP BREATH, HOLDS HER NOSE, THEN KISSES HIM. SUDDENLY, SHE DROPS HER HAND AND STEPS BACK IN AMAZEMENT, AS IF A HANDSOME PRINCE HAS JUST APPEARED.) Oh, wow! Oh, wow, wow, wow! Oh, wow, wow, wow, wow, WOW! My fairy godmother sure knows her stuff! You really *did* turn into a handsome prince!

(FLIRTATIOUSLY) So, what do you say, gorgeous? Do you want to go for a drive? Take in a movie? Get married?

(SHE PRETENDS TO TAKE HIS ARM AND STARTS TO WALK OFFSTAGE. THEN, ALL OF A SUDDEN, SHE STOPS.)

But, first, (SHE LOOKS HIM OVER.) suck in that belly! Stand up straight! Hold back those shoulders! And honestly, if you think you're spending the rest of your life with me, Buster, you've *really* got to do something about those unsightly warts!

(SHE WALKS OFFSTAGE MUMBLING MORE INSTRUCTIONS.)

BLACKOUT

"No, thanks. I just flossed."

Snow White's Sweet Temptation

CHARACTER: Snow White

SETTING: The Seven Dwarfs' cottage

PROPS: Broom
Dirty sock on floor

COSTUME: Fairy tale type dress

SOUND EFFECTS: Doorbell

(SNOW WHITE IS SWEEPING THE LIVING ROOM OF THE COTTAGE.)

(STOPPING JUST LONG ENOUGH TO CATCH HER BREATH) Whew! They may be little, but those seven dwarfs can sure mess up a cottage! I tell you, I work my fingers to the bone around here. I make all their little beds, cook all their little meals, iron all their little clothes, and what do I get for it? Back cramps from trying to fit through all their little doors!

Oh, I realize I should be thanking them for hiding me from that wicked Queen, but I can't go on like this. I've got a life to live! I've got dreams! I've got ambitions! I've got . . . (SNEEZES) an allergy to something in this forest!

(DOORBELL RINGS, BUT SNOW WHITE CONTINUES TALKING.) But, don't get me wrong. It's not that I don't like it here. But . . . (BENDS OVER AND PICKS UP DIRTY SOCK) you try picking up ninety-eight dirty socks every week. Frankly (SHE BRINGS THE SOCK UP TO HER NOSE AND TAKES A WHIFF, THEN GRIMACES.), this is *not* my idea of living happily ever after!

(DOORBELL RINGS AGAIN.) All right, all right, I'm coming! (SHE SETS THE BROOM DOWN, WALKS OVER TO THE SIDE OF THE STAGE AND MIMES OPENING THE DOOR.) Look, whatever it is you're selling, I don't want any. I've already bought twelve raffle tickets from Little Leaguers, 26 magazine subscriptions from the PTA, and 108 "HAVE A LOUSY DAY" buttons from Grumpy's Bad Attitude Club. So, kindly peddle your goods elsewhere!

. . . What's that? You say you're not selling anything. You just want to give me a nice shiny apple? . . . Well, I have been working up quite an appetite. (SHE MIMES TAKING THE APPLE AND BRINGS IT TO HER LIPS. BUT JUST AS SHE'S ABOUT TO TAKE A BITE, SHE STOPS.) No, I'd better not. I just flossed. (SHE STARTS TO HAND IT BACK TO HER, BUT HESITATES.) . . . But then again, apples *are* good for you. (SHE STARTS TO TAKE A BITE AGAIN, BUT ONCE AGAIN STOPS.) But now, they're even better in a strudel! . . . You wouldn't happen to have anything like that in your basket, would you? . . . No? . . . Well, check your pockets. I have a mean sweet tooth! I'll take anything—French apple pie, apple turnovers, apple danish. (BRIEF PAUSE) . . . Nothing, huh?

. . . Wait! I know what I'll do. I'll call the Castle Bakery. They deliver. I'll order four apple turnovers, seven apple muffins, two dozen apple cookies, three apple danish, six apple fritters, a French apple pie, 5 candied apples, and a . . .

. . . What's that? . . . Aren't I going to eat the apple you brought? (SHE PRETENDS TO LOOK OVER THE APPLE IN HER HAND.) What? And spoil my dinner?! (SHE MIMES HANDING THE APPLE BACK TO THE VISITOR AND SHUTS THE DOOR.)

BLACKOUT

"Rapunzel, Rapunzel, let down your hair. The guys and I want to have a tug o' war."

A Very Hairy Situation

CHARACTER: Rapunzel

SETTING: Beauty salon counter

PROPS: Sign that says "DEN O'DANDRUFF BEAUTY SALON"

COSTUME: Fairy tale type dress
A braided wig that reaches the floor and beyond

(RAPUNZEL IS STANDING AT THE BEAUTY SALON COUNTER. THE "DEN O'DANDRUFF" SIGN IS ON THE COUNTER. RAPUNZEL, PERTURBED, IS TALKING TO THE IMAGINARY CLERK.)

What do you mean "four hundred and sixty-three dollars"? All I want is a shampoo and set, not your beauty salon lease!

(TO AUDIENCE) Boy, I tell you, it's not easy having hair this long. Kids are always wanting to use it for a jump rope! They tie a ball to the end of it and play tetherball! And every time they see me in pigtails, they choose up sides for a game of tug o' war!

And those aren't the only drawbacks. I

can't use regular shampoo like "Head and Shoulders." I've got to special order "Head and Feet."

And it's affecting my love life, too. The last time I let a guy run his fingers through my hair, he didn't get back for a week and a half!

But, I think that part of my luck's changing now. You see, there's this fella who's been using my braid to climb up to the top of the tower where I live. . . . You've heard of guys getting in your hair? Well, this guy does it literally! In fact, that's why I need a shampoo so badly. This hair's seen more footprints than Grauman's Chinese Theatre!

(TURNING BACK TO IMAGINARY CLERK) So, what do you say? Can you give me a break on the price? I promise to recommend you to all my friends—Snow White, Sleeping Beauty, Cinderella. I'll even get Rip Van Winkle in here to let you give him a shave. The guy's got a five o'clock shadow you would not believe!

So, how about it? . . . What? You say you will? Hey, that's terrific!

Oh, and can you hurry? I've got to get back before that cute boy comes looking for my braid again. I mean, let's face it, if he ever discovers the tower has an elevator, there go my Saturday nights!

BLACKOUT

HOLIDAY
MONOLOGUES

"I want the correct answer, Abe. And no more of your 'fourscore and seven' stuff!"

The Ideal Class President

CHARACTER: A young Abraham Lincoln

SETTING: Inside Abe's one-room schoolhouse

PROPS: Posters on the wall that say: "VOTE 4 ABE", "ABE'S A BABE", and "ABE LINCOLN FOR CLASS PRESIDENT"

COSTUME: Even though he's a young Lincoln, he should still look the part (beard, hat, suit, etc.).

(LINCOLN IS STANDING CENTER STAGE GIVING A SPEECH.)

Fellow classmates . . . fourscore and seven recesses ago I decided to toss my stovepipe hat into the ring and run for class president.

Why? Because I want to serve my fellow students. I want to make a difference at this school. And frankly, until my dad lets me start shaving, what else do I have to do?

Now, I realize this is a small school—only one classroom to be exact—but we still need leadership, we still need direction, and we still need indoor plumbing, but first things first.

So, if you're tired of using inkwells that make flicking your Bic take an hour-and-a-half, vote for Abe!

If you're fed up with our school assemblies being disrupted by Indian attacks, or even worse—rowdy ninth graders, then I'm your guy!

If you've grown weary of having to play animal soccer with *real* buffalo . . . and you know how *they* cheat . . . then cast your ballot for Abraham Lincoln!

Friends, I love this school. But to make it an even better place, I've outlined some concrete proposals.

. . . And speaking of concrete, we'll talk about cafeteria food first. Now, everyone knows I'm the best log-splitter in the country, but even *my* ax can't make it through one of their submarine sandwiches!

But if I'm elected president, I promise to change all that. We'll have sandwiches softer than our school books, and tacos tastier than our tennies!

And I won't stop there! You want more hitching posts? You got 'em! You want more field trips to Mount Rushmore? They're yours! . . . Even though there are just the two heads there now. But they'll be adding to it someday.

So, go ahead, make my political career and vote for *Abraham Lincoln*! You'll be glad you did! (RAISING HIS ARM, VOWING) . . . Honest!

BLACKOUT

"Of course, he loves me! Do you think he'd invert his eyelids, shoot spitwads, and make that funny noise with his armpit for just anybody?!"

Cupid Gets the Point

CHARACTER: Cupid

SETTING: The "Arrows R Us" School of Archery

PROPS: Free-standing counter
Sign that says " 'ARROWS R US' SCHOOL OF ARCHERY"
Target
Bow and arrows, with pouch (For safety reasons, arrows should have rubber suction tips)

COSTUME: Cupid outfit (pink leotards, tights, wings, etc.)

(CUPID RUSHES IN AND APPROACHES THE COUNTER, LOCATED CENTER STAGE. HE CARRIES THE BOW IN HIS HAND. AND WEARS THE POUCH FULL OF ARROWS ON HIS BACK. THE SIGN IS IN CLEAR VIEW OF THE AUDIENCE. THE TARGET IS HANGING ON A WALL BEHIND THE COUNTER.)

(TO IMAGINARY CLERK) You've got to help me! If I don't improve my aim, and do it *quickly*, I'm out of a job!

. . . My name? It's Cupid. (SPELLING IT) C-U-P-I-D. (DEFENSIVE) Hey, it wasn't *my* idea! I wanted "Rocky." But then, how many Rockys do you see dressed like this, huh?

Anyway, getting back to my crisis—do you think you could help me work on my aim? (HE REACHES INTO HIS POUCH AND PULLS OUT AN ARROW. TAKING AIM, HE SHOOTS IT BUT MISSES THE TARGET COMPLETELY.)

You see, I'm in the matchmaking business. Why, romance is my middle name. . . . I would have preferred "Killer" for a middle name, but again, the outfit held me back.

But let me get right to the point. Last Valentine's Day, my bad aim caused a lot of problems—you know, mismatches, that sort of thing. (HE PULLS OUT ANOTHER ARROW AND SHOOTS, BUT IT, TOO, MISSES THE TARGET.) Why, would you believe I matched a giraffe with a laughing hyena? Naturally, it didn't work out. He kept wanting to neck. But she just couldn't get serious about him.

(HE SHOOTS AGAIN AND MISSES.) And I matched a pig with an elephant. That didn't work out either. She got tired of always bringing home the bacon while he just sat at home and watched Dumbo reruns. She finally told him to pack up his trunk and get out!

(HE SHOOTS AGAIN AND ONCE MORE MISSES.) And that chihuahua-rhinoceros match didn't turn out any better. As soon as the chihuahua carried the rhino over the threshold, that marriage was over. She left him flat!

So, you see, you've just got to help me! Cupid losing his aim is like Santa Claus developing a fear of flying! It's like the Easter Bunny discovering he's allergic to eggs!

Look, I promise I'll try really hard! I'll be your best student! (HE PREPARES ANOTHER ARROW TO SHOOT.) I'll . . . (HE SHOOTS IT, THEN GASPS.) Oh, I'm so sorry! I didn't mean for it to hit you. Please forgive . . . (STARTS TO BACK AWAY) Uh-oh. Why are you looking at me with that gleam in your eye? (NERVOUSLY) Uh . . . uh . . . I don't think you understand. It was just an accident. Besides, I'm already going with someone else. Yeah, my wings were clipped long ago. . . . So, c'mon now, stay back. Stay back or I'll . . . (HE GRABS ANOTHER ARROW FROM HIS POUCH AND SHOOTS IN HER DIRECTION.) Oh, great. Now, I've hit your assistant. And she's getting that same look in her eye! (HE SHOOTS ANOTHER ARROW, THEN GULPS.) . . . Oh, no, not your cleaning lady, too! (HE SHOOTS

ARROW AFTER ARROW WHILE BACKING AWAY, NERVOUSLY.) Uh . . . maybe it's time I looked into a career change.

But then again . . . (HE STANDS UP TALL, STRAIGHTENS HIS OUTFIT, BRUSHES BACK HIS HAIR WITH HIS HAND.) . . . when you've got it, you've got it! (HE PUTS HIS ARMS OUT AS IF WANTING THE GIRLS TO TAKE THEM, THEN STRUTS OFFSTAGE.)

BLACKOUT

A Bunny 4 Hire

CHARACTER: The Easter Bunny

SETTING: The "Get To Work" Employment Agency

PROPS: A sign that says "The Get To Work Employment Agency"
A counter with papers and phone on it
Business card

COSTUME: Easter Bunny outfit (the business card should be concealed somewhere in the outfit)

(THE EASTER BUNNY IS STANDING AT THE COUNTER. HE'S A TAD FRUSTRATED, TO SAY THE LEAST.)

(TO IMAGINARY CLERK) Look, don't give me a hard time. All I want is a little extra work . . . for the off-season. This Easter Bunny gig isn't exactly year-round employment, you know. I've got bills to pay! I've got my future to think about! Bugs Bunny

"All right, who's been hiding all the eggs?"

doesn't have to worry about his retirement years. He's got residuals. But what do I have to show for a lifetime of hippety hopping? (SHOWING OFF HIS FEET) Blisters! Nothing but blisters!

. . . What's that? You say I'm in the wrong line? . . . But I had to wait in this line twenty minutes! . . . Oh, I see. You say the right line always takes twenty-five.

(HE MOVES ON DOWN THE COUNTER AS IF TO ANOTHER CLERK.) Hi. I hope you can help me. I'm looking for a part-time job. Tell me, could you use someone with excellent typing skills? . . . You could? . . . Well, so could I . . . to type out my memoirs!

Or perhaps you have need of a good bodyguard? . . . Yes? . . . Well, I could sure use one, too. I tell you, when you've got biceps like these (HE FLEXES HIS ARM MUSCLES.), the girls just won't leave you alone!

. . . What's that? . . . You'd like to know exactly what type of job skills I do possess? Well, (HE THINKS FOR A MOMENT.) I can hide Easter eggs. And . . . (THINKS FOR ANOTHER MOMENT) I can hide Easter eggs. And . . . (THINKS FOR YET ANOTHER MOMENT) . . . Uh, did I mention I can hide Easter eggs? . . . Okay, I admit it, I'm a specialist!

. . . But, hey, wait, I know something I

could do. I could substitute for other holiday symbols. Yes, Santa Claus would probably love some time off. I'll quit shaving, put on a few pounds. No one will know the difference!

Or how about Cupid? I've got good aim (HE MIMES SHOOTING AN ARROW.), and I look great in pink tights!

. . . Well, look (HANDS OVER HIS BUSINESS CARD), here's my business card. If anything comes up, just give me a call.

In the meantime, I guess I'd better get back to hiding my Easter eggs. Like I said, I'm only working one day a year right now, but, boy oh boy, it can really keep me hopping! (AS HE HOPS OFFSTAGE, HE TURNS BACK.) Happy Easter! (EXITS)

BLACKOUT

Columbus's Big Discovery

CHARACTER: Columbus
SETTING: Deck of a ship
PROPS: Telescope
COSTUME: Sea-faring clothes (or to put it another way—Queen Isabella designer beachware)

(COLUMBUS IS STANDING CENTER STAGE, TELESCOPE IN HAND. HE TAKES A FEW STEPS TO THE RIGHT AND LOOKS THROUGH THE TELE-SCOPE. HE TAKES A FEW STEPS TO THE LEFT AND LOOKS THROUGH THE TELESCOPE. THEN, HE SHRUGS HIS SHOULDERS, LOWERS THE TELE-SCOPE, AND LOOKS TOWARD THE AUDIENCE.)

All right, so maybe I was wrong. Maybe the world *is* flat, and I'm about to sail off the edge of it.

"We agree America's a lovely place, Columbus. But your cruise brochure said 'India.'"

I mean, whatever made me think it was round in the first place? An instinct? A feeling? A postcard from Hawaii?

(HE TAKES ANOTHER LOOK THROUGH THE TELESCOPE, THEN SHAKES HIS HEAD.) But, hey, I knew it was chancy when I started out on this journey aboard Exploration Cruise Lines. Still, I wanted to try. (HE BEGINS PACING.) I wanted to know if my suspicions were correct. I wanted to know if indeed the world is round or if . . . (HE STOPS AND LOOKS STRAIGHT AT THE AUDIENCE.) . . . I'm going to be stuck with those 5,000 world globes I've got stashed in my garage!

(HE BEGINS PACING AGAIN.) That's why I asked Queen Isabella to lend me three ships—The Pinta, The Nina, and The Santa Maria, and I told her not to hold dinner on us.

. . . And speaking of dinner . . . (HE TAKES A FEW STEPS AND PRETENDS TO BE LOOKING INTO THE SHIP'S GALLEY.) We appear to be running low on food. (HE LOOKS OUT TOWARD AUDIENCE AGAIN.) Oh, don't get me wrong. We've managed to ration the staples. It's just that all the *good* food is gone. I mean, we're down to Marlin Helper three meals a day now. Boy, what I wouldn't give for some nachos!

(SUDDENLY, HE EYES SOMETHING OFF TO HIS RIGHT.) Wait a minute! (HE

LIFTS THE TELESCOPE TO HIS EYE.) That looks like land over there! (HE FOCUSES THE TELESCOPE.) Yes! Yes! It is land! (HE LOWERS THE TELESCOPE, THEN SHOUTS OFFSTAGE TO HIS CREW.) Land Ho! Land Ho!

(HE BEGINS PACING, EXCITEDLY.) I can't believe this! I was right all along! The world isn't flat! It's round! And just as soon as we dock, I'm going to call the Queen and tell her what I've found! Man, oh, man, this is really going to make her day!

(HE STOPS ABRUPTLY.) But, wait a second! What's the matter with me? I can't *call* anyone. Not *yet* anyway! (HE LOOKS OUT AT THE AUDIENCE AND SMILES.) Everyone knows it's cheaper after six!

BLACKOUT

The Great Turkey Uprising

CHARACTER: The Turkey Union President

SETTING: Boardroom with signs that say "TURKEYS UNITE" and "THANKSGIVING DAY MENU UNFAIR TO TURKEYS!"

PROPS: Lectern
Bunny ears (on lectern but out of view of audience)

COSTUME: Turkey costume

And so, distinguished friends, honored guests, and all the rest of you turkeys, I say it's time we get up off our tailfeathers and stand up for our rights! I say it's time we tell them to take their stuffing and stuff it! I say it's time we strike!

"It's an invitation to their
Thanksgiving Day feast! Now, aren't
you ashamed you were so suspicious
of those Pilgrims?"

Who made us the traditional Thanksgiving entree anyway? The food editor from the *New York Times* wasn't at that first Thanksgiving feast, so how can we be sure the pilgrims didn't serve Sloppy Joes? I mean—just because they've discovered over 300 recipes for leftover turkey drawn on the walls of old Indian caves, that still doesn't prove anything.

. . . Uh, Tom, I notice you're raising your wing. Do you have a question or are you just testing your anti-perspirant?

. . . What's that? You say we should be proud of our standing in society? . . . Hey, we don't have any problem with our standing. It's when they ask us to lay prostrate on a platter that makes us a little nervous!

. . . And, you say we should be happy we're able to bring a little joy, love, and togetherness to families everywhere? . . . Look, baggy nose, the only togetherness I'm interested in is keeping my drumsticks together with the rest of me!

So, how about it, gang? Are you with me? Will our song be "United We Stand" or will it be "Home, Home in the Microwave"?

. . . *Now* what is it, Tom? . . . Yes, I realize if it wasn't for us, some people would never remember to say thanks for all they've been given. So, hey, let them go roast Miss Manners. Why do *we* have to get involved?

. . . Wait a minute, where are you all

going? Why's everyone leaving with Tom? Can't you see he's just afraid to stand up for his rights? Why, he's not a turkey. He's a chicken! So, c'mon, stay here with me and we'll show them what we're made of! We'll show them when they mess with us, they're biting off more than they can chew! . . . Uh, perhaps I should rephrase that . . .

. . . So, that's it, huh? You're leaving anyway? You're giving up your dignity, your self-respect, your wishbones—just so people can sit around on Thanksgiving and eat themselves into a poultry coma?

. . . All right, fine. Go ahead. But as for me . . . (HE PUTS ON THE BUNNY EARS.) . . . I'm moving to a safer holiday! (EXITS)

BLACKOUT

Heave, Ho, Ho, Ho

CHARACTER: Santa Claus

SETTING: A rooftop with chimney

PROPS: A free-standing brick chimney
A bag full of toys, set off to the side of chimney

COSTUME: Santa suit

(SANTA IS STUCK INSIDE THE CHIMNEY AND TRYING TO WORK HIMSELF LOOSE.)

Now, *this* is embarrassing! (HE STRUGGLES A BIT MORE, BUT IS STILL STUCK.) I knew I never should have dropped out of that Elfs Aerobics class, but you try doing 150 jumping jacks in a velvet suit and knee boots! I tell you, it's no picnic! And besides, I didn't appreciate Rudolph giggling everytime he saw me in leotards!

(HE TRIES WORKING HIS WAY OUT AGAIN, BUT EVERY EFFORT ONLY SEEMS TO WORSEN HIS PREDICAMENT.)

"Maybe it's time I started going door-to-door!"

Look, it's not as though I don't watch what I eat. I do. (A BEAT) All right, I admit I cheat a little every Christmas Eve by eating three billion or so cookies, but from then on it's alfalfa sprouts and celery all the way!

(HE TRIES TO FREE HIMSELF AGAIN. BUT ONCE AGAIN, HE CAN'T.) Oh, what's taking those reindeer so long? I just sent them down to the local mini-mart for some Vaseline to see if that will help, but they must have gotten sidetracked by the video games.

(HE LOOKS OFF TO THE SIDE.) Hey, wait a minute! Here comes a helicopter! Maybe he'll help me! (CUPPING HIS HAND, HE CALLS OUT.) Yahoo! Hey, you up there! This is Santa Claus and I'm stuck in this chimney! Can you help me? . . . What's that? . . . Well, the same to you, buddy! (TO AUDIENCE) Forget one little thing on their Christmas list and they never forget, do they?

(ONCE AGAIN HE TRIES TO GET LOOSE BUT FAILS.) I suppose I should have listened to my reindeer when they first started complaining about pulling the extra weight. Dancer and Prancer wanted to change their names to Draggin' and Laggin', and Rudolph claimed the added stress was giving him high blood pressure. He said that's why his nose is always so red!

And now they're threatening to strike if I don't hire four more reindeer. Imagine—four more! Why, do you realize what that's going to cost me in health insurance, workman's comp, and retirement benefits, not to mention the expense of adding their names to the "The Night Before Christmas" poem?

I suppose the best thing for me to do is simply get back into shape. Yeah, I'll take up Arctic jogging, glacier climbing, and ice golfing. I'll. . . .

(SUDDENLY) Hey, wait a minute! Wait a minute! I think I just felt myself move! Yes! Yes! I'm finally breaking loose! (HE REACHES OVER AND GRABS THE BAG OF TOYS; AND AS THEY BOTH DISAPPEAR INTO THE CHIMNEY, HE YELLS.) Merrrrrryyyy Chrissssstttt-mmmaaaasssss! (THERE'S A BRIEF PAUSE, THEN FROM INSIDE THE CHIMNEY WE HEAR. . . .)

I just hope the next house has a sun roof!

BLACKOUT

HISTORICAL
MONOLOGUES

"Ben, don't you think you're a little old for a punk hair-do?"

Ben's Shocking Experiment

CHARACTER:	Ben Franklin
SETTING:	Ben's living room (with front door)
PROPS:	Kite with string and key attached
	Envelope (kept inside Ben's vest pocket)
COSTUME:	Knee pants, shirt, vest
	"Ben Franklin" style glasses
SPECIAL EFFECTS:	Stage lights that can be flashed on and off

(BEN, HOLDING HIS KITE, PREPARES TO STEP OUT FOR THE EVENING.)

(TO WIFE, UNSEEN BY AUDIENCE)
I'll be going outside for a while now, dear. . . .
Yes, I *know* it's raining. . . . And, yes, I

realize it's thundering and lightning, too. But I've got to keep working on my experiment. After all, until I discover electricity, what good's the television set?

(STARTS TOWARD DOOR, THEN STOPS) . . . What's that, dear? . . . You want me to take out the garbage . . . But, sweetheart, don't you realize the sooner I discover electricity, the sooner we can use that trash compactor I got you for Valentine's Day?

(HE STARTS TOWARD THE DOOR AGAIN, BUT ONCE MORE STOPS.) . . . *Now* what is it? . . . No, I haven't forgotten about those shelves you want me to put up. But once I discover electricity, I'll be able to use my electric power drill and hang them up in a flash. . . . And speaking of flash, I'd better get out there before this storm passes. You see, this storm is *very* important to my experiment. Without the lightning, I'd have to write all my notes in the dark!

(STARTS TO EXIT ONCE MORE, BUT STOPS) What is it *this* time? . . . You want to know why I'm taking along this kite? . . . Oh, that's just in case I don't discover anything. I've got to have something to do out there.

Now then, don't bother me anymore. I'm going to go out there and conduct my experiment, and if my calculations are correct, our new can-opener will be operational by dinnertime! (HE MIMES

OPENING THE DOOR, THEN RAISES HIS HAND IN A GESTURE OF CONFIDENCE.) To the dawn of a new age! (HE EXITS OFFSTAGE. THE STAGE LIGHTS FLASH ON AND OFF. OFFSTAGE, WE HEAR BEN YELL.) Yeeoowww!

(BEN REENTERS, OUT OF BREATH. HIS HAIR IS STANDING ON END AND HIS CLOTHES ARE IN DISARRAY) Uhhh, dear . . . you'd better stick with the pop-top cans for awhile. You see, my experiment worked. I did discover electricity. But the real "shock" came when I got this. (HE REACHES INTO HIS VEST POCKET AND BRINGS OUT AN ENVELOPE.) . . . Our first electric bill!

"It's nice, Betsy, but your class
assignment was to make a gym bag."

Betsy's Big Order

CHARACTER: Betsy Ross

SETTING: Betsy Ross's Upholstery Shop and Drive-Thru Boutique

PROPS: "BETSY ROSS'S UPHOLSTERY SHOP AND DRIVE-THRU BOUTIQUE" sign
Service counter
Order pad
Quill pen
Large advertising pictures of: wingback chair and butter churner

COSTUMES: Revolutionary era clothing

(BETSY, BEHIND THE COUNTER, IS BUSY FILLING OUT AN ORDER FORM. SHE STOPS AND LOOKS UP AS IF TALKING TO A CUSTOMER.)

Now, General Washington, let me see if I've got this correct. You want me to sew a flag that has (READING FROM ORDER FORM) thirteen stripes, alternately red and white, with a union of thirteen stars of white on a blue field? (LOOKS UP) I couldn't interest you in a tea towel with two duckies on a grassy plain instead, huh?

Or perhaps this (HOLDS UP PICTURE OF THE WINGBACK CHAIR) lovely wingback recliner for the laidback aristocrat.

Or how about this (HOLDS UP PICTURE OF BUTTER CHURNER) state-of-the-art electric butter churner? Now I admit since electricity hasn't been invented yet, finding an outlet is going to be a bit tricky; but hey, when it's a bargain like this, who cares?

What's that? You say you just want the flag and that's it? . . . Well, all right, but just how soon will you be needing it? Right away?! Say, what do I look like to you? A Singer Zig Zag with hair? I do all this work by hand, you know. It takes time. And time is money. And speaking of money, how much are you willing to pay? . . .Fourteen pounds? Why, that's barely enough to cover the wear and tear on my thimble!

Look, maybe you should go down to the local Flags R Us, buy a kit and let your wife sew it. . . . You say she wanted to, but you don't consider flag-making her specialty? . . . C'mon, how bad could she be? . . . Well, yes, you're right, most flags *don't* have sleeves.

. . . So, fourteen pounds is the highest you can go, huh? (THINKS FOR A

MOMENT) Well, I can't exactly open up a C.D. on that kind of money, but—okay—I'll take the job.

Now then, General Washington, how were you planning on paying for this? Cash? Check? Your Colonial Express Card? . . . You say you left Mount Vernon without it? . . . Very well, cash will be fine. (SHE JOTS DOWN A FEW SCRIBBLINGS ON THE ORDER FORM.) Well, I suppose that takes care of everything. (SHE TEARS THE ORDER FORM OUT OF THE PAD AND SLIDES IT ACROSS THE COUNTER TOWARD HIM.) And don't worry, sir. I'll get on it right away. I know how important this flag is to all of us.

But, sir, before you go, I'd like to ask just one more question. How did your wife take it when you told her you were giving the job to someone else? . . . Really? You say she understood completely? In fact, to prove there were no hard feelings she sewed you that shirt you're wearing right now? . . . Why, wasn't that nice? But next time, sir, tell her to remember the hole to put your head through!

BLACKOUT

"Okay, Orville, so maybe it is *too big* to enter in the school science fair."

Orville's Show and Tell

CHARACTER: Orville Wright
SETTING: Orville and Wilbur's
               schoolroom
PROPS: None needed
COSTUME: Aviator type clothing from
               that era (goggles, scarf,
               etc.)

(ORVILLE IS STANDING CENTER
STAGE.)

(LOOKING TOWARD THE AUDIENCE
AS THOUGH THEY WERE A
CLASSROOM FULL OF STUDENTS)
Hello, class. My brother Wilbur and I have
been working very hard on our project for the
science fair this year. (HE TURNS AND
CALLS OFFSTAGE.) All right, Wilbur, you
can bring 'er on in. (DUCKING QUICKLY)
Whoa! I said "*bring* 'er in", not . . . (DUCKS
AGAIN) . . . "*fly* 'er in"! Now land that thing
before we're both assigned a three-hour

layover in the principal's office! (COAXING) That's it. Bring her down slowly. Careful. Careful. (SIGH OF RELIEF) Ah, a perfect landing! . . . Well, *almost* perfect. You probably shouldn't have landed on our teacher. (TO IMAGINARY TEACHER) But don't worry, Miss Marsh. Those treadmarks should come off with a little soap and water.

(TO AUDIENCE) Now then, class, this is what my brother and I call the "airplane." We were going to call it the "Harley-Davidson," but no matter how hard we tried, we could never get it to pop a wheelie!

Another reason we call it the airplane is because it goes up into the air. You've already seen how it can do that. (ASIDE) No, no, Wilbur. Don't take it up again. I'm sure with thirty kids in this room, Miss Marsh sees enough things sailing through the air! In fact, since our last demonstration of the "paper airplane," I believe half the class is on the Frequent Flyer program!

(TO AUDIENCE) Now then, allow me to point out some of the different parts of the airplane. (DEMONSTRATING) You'll notice the airplane has two wings. We tried making it with only one, but all it did was go around in circles. It was all right with us, but it sure made our stewardess dizzy!

(ASIDE TO WILBUR) Uh, Wilbur, whatever you do, don't touch that red button over there.

(CONTINUING TO POINT OUT THE VARIOUS PARTS TO THE AUDIENCE) Now, this here is the cockpit. And this is the rear rudder. And this is the landing gear. . . . I wish you could get a better view of the landing gear, but unfortunately, Miss Marsh is still attached to it.

(ASIDE TO WILBUR) I *said* don't touch that red button!

(TURNING BACK TO AUDIENCE) Now, you may be wondering what's so great about air travel. Well, the advantages are endless. Just think—no more running to catch the Good Humor truck, no more tardies for school, and imagine how easy it'd be to steal second base in one of these babies! Yes, fellow students, we just might be on the threshold of a brand new era, an era of. . . .

(ABRUPT TURN TOWARD IMAGINARY WILBUR) Wilbur! I said don't touch that . . . (HE LOOKS UP AND ROLLS HIS EYES AS IF FOLLOWING AN AIRBORNE WILBUR.) Well, as you can see, that button controlled the ejection seat! But it's all right. He wanted to go home for lunch anyway!

BLACKOUT

"Look, I'll say it one more time. It's 'one if by land, two if by sea, and three if they're coming by Lamborghini!'"

The British Are Coming . . . And They Didn't Even R.S.V.P.

CHARACTER: Paul Revere
SETTING: Countryside
PROPS: Stick horse
Road map
COSTUME: Revolutionary era costume

(PAUL ENTERS, RIDING THE STICK HORSE. THE MAP IS TUCKED AWAY IN HIS POCKET.)

(TO AUDIENCE) When I told the salesman I wanted a Mustang convertible, this wasn't exactly what I had in mind! (SHRUGS SHOULDERS) Oh, well. . . .

(TO HORSE) Giddy up! (THE HORSE DOESN'T BUDGE.) C'mon, boy, giddy up! (STILL THE HORSE DOESN'T MOVE. PAUL TURNS TO AUDIENCE) And he wonders why I don't enter him in the Kentucky Derby!

(PATTING TAIL OF STICK) C'mon, quit being an ol' stick in the mud—uh, no offense—but we've got to get moving. I have to warn all the colonists that the redcoats are coming. And you know how we all hate unexpected company!

So, c'mon. (THE HORSE REARS BACK, WITH THE HELP OF OUR STAR, OF COURSE, AND THEY START GALLOPING AROUND THE STAGE.) That's it! That's a good boy! (THEY GALLOP A FEW MORE STEPS, THEN BOUNCE UP IN THE AIR, AND GALLOP A FEW MORE STEPS. HE EXPLAINS TO THE AUDIENCE.) Speed bump.

Okay, now, let's get to work! (THEY GALLOP AROUND THE STAGE AS PAUL BEGINS TO YELL) The redcoats are coming! The redcoats are coming! (LOUDER) The redcoats are coming! The redcoats are coming! (LOUDER STILL) The redcoats are coming! The redcoats are coming! (OUT OF BREATH NOW, HE STOPS AND LOOKS OUT TOWARD THE AUDIENCE.) Boy, I tell you, where's a Mr. Microphone when you need it, huh?

Oh, well, if the people don't hear me, surely they'll see the church light. You see, I've got a signal all worked out. It's (COUNTING OFF ON HIS FINGERS) "one if by land, two if by sea, and three if they're coming by Lamborghini! Four if by taxi, five if by bus, and six if they're planning to skateboard to us! Seven if by pogo-stick, eight if by . . ."—well, you get the idea.

Now then, which way do I go from here? (HE TAKES THE MAP FROM HIS POCKET AND UNFOLDS IT.) Ummm . . . I just finished warning everyone on Ben Franklin Circle. And I did all the condos on George Washington Way. . . . Or was that the Jefferson Avenue townhouses that I just did? (STUDYING MAP) Wait a minute! Wait a minute! I know *exactly* where I am now. (HE RUNS HIS FINGER ALONG THE MAP AS IF CALCULATING HIS WHEREABOUTS. HE THEN LOOKS OUT TOWARD AUDIENCE AND NODS.) . . . I'm lost!

But, not to worry! I'll just fold up this map and follow my natural sense of direction. (HE TRIES FOLDING THE MAP, BUT IT DOESN'T WANT TO BE FOLDED.) Yes, I'll just fold up this map and follow my instincts! (HE TRIES IT AGAIN, BUT ONCE AGAIN FAILS.) I'll just fold up this map and follow my own intuition! (HE ATTEMPTS IT ONCE MORE, BUT THE MAP JUST WON'T REFOLD.) I'll just leave this map here and let the redcoats try to figure it out! (HE TOSSES IT ASIDE.) That ought to stall them for a week or two! And believe me, I could use the extra time to notify the rest of the colonists.

(HE STARTS TO RIDE OFFSTAGE.) The redcoats are coming! The redcoats are coming! (HE STOPS AND TURNS TO AUDIENCE.) I mean, let's face it, if Peter Jennings had to work like this, you'd never get your news!

(AS HE RIDES OFFSTAGE, WE HEAR HIS WARNING FADING IN THE DISTANCE.) The redcoats are coming! The redcoats are coming! The redcoats. . . .

BLACKOUT

MONOLOGUE
GRAB BAG

"*Maybe volleyball isn't the game for you, George.*"

The Minor, Minor League Draft

CHARACTER: Boy or girl
SETTING: School playground
PROPS: None needed
COSTUME: Ordinary clothing
Baseball cap, worn
backwards

(OUR STAR STANDS CENTER STAGE, LOOKING A LITTLE GLUM.)

Well, here we go again. It's team selection day, and as usual, I'll be the last one picked. Nobody ever wants me on their team. (SIGHS) I feel like a chip on the bowling ball of life! A wad of chewing gum on the Reeboks of humanity! A speed bump on the football field of mankind.

Tony will get picked first, of course. After all, he's the best player in the whole school. Or, at least, that's what he had printed on his T-shirt!

And Carla will get selected because she's such a fast runner. If nobody picks her, she can be home in 83 seconds to tell her big brother!

Yessir, I might as well face it. I'm going to be standing here till Halley's Comet comes back!

. . . Aw, I guess I don't really blame them. I mean, who wants a player on their team who runs around the bases so slowly, he (OR SHE) takes along a sleeping bag? Or someone who couldn't catch a fly if they had a No-Pest Strip hanging around their neck! Or someone who . . .

(STOPS SUDDENLY AND LOOKS AROUND) Hey, wait a minute! Did I just hear Matthew calling out my name for his team? . . . And look, now Rusty's waving me over to *her* team, too. This is sure strange. I wonder what the odds are of *both* team captains being delirious at the same time?

(BRIEFLY THINKING IT OVER) But, then again, I *have* been making some dramatic improvements lately on the soccerfield. I can now play most of the game in the upright position! And my volleyball skills have greatly improved. I haven't gotten tangled up in the net all semester!

Yep! That's got to be it! They've seen my potential, and they know what I'm capable of!

They've finally come to appreciate my ever-increasing athletic abilities! They recognize a budding Olympic star when they see one!

And then, of course, it just might have something to do with the fact that this year (SMILES BROADLY) . . . my mom's bringing the refreshments!

BLACKOUT

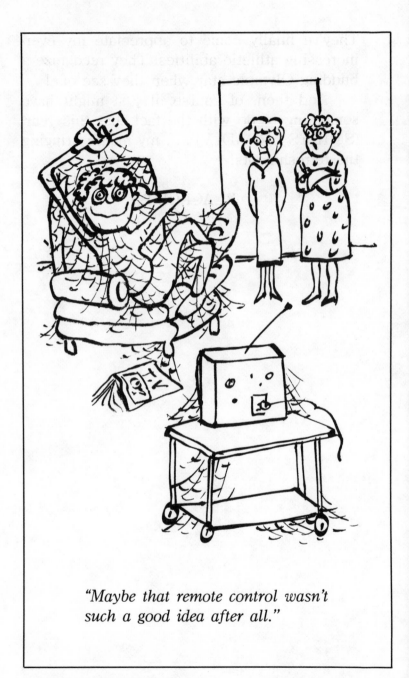

"Maybe that remote control wasn't
such a good idea after all."

For the Love of T.V.

CHARACTER: Boy or girl television set
SETTING: No set needed
PROPS: None needed
COSTUME: Black tights and a box that makes our star look like a television set. We should be able to see our star's face through the screen portion of the set.

(OUR LIVE TELEVISION SET STANDS CENTER STAGE, LOOKING OUT TOWARD THE AUDIENCE)

Look, honey, we need to talk. We've got to stop meeting like this—the two of us . . . together every morning, noon, and night. It's no good.

But now, don't get me wrong. I still love it when you whisper sweet nothings into my remote control and run your fingers through my antennae. It's just that I need some time to myself.

Oh, c'mon, now. Don't cry. Goodness knows, I get enough tears from my soap operas. And besides, if you start crying, I'll start crying, and you wouldn't want my insides to rust, would you? . . . You say since I'm the one breaking up, that might not be such a bad idea?

Hey, come on. You'll survive without me. You've done it before. Why, remember that blackout we had last fall? You live through it. . . . Of course, I was only out of your sight for fifteen minutes, and even then they had to give you emergency Cosby transfusions, but you made it. And when we got back together, we appreciated each other even more.

And listen, you're free to see other entertainment sources while we're apart. Go ahead, read a good book, go to a play, visit a museum. I won't get jealous. I realize I can't be your whole life.

See, it's just that I don't want our relationship to become static. I want to be special to you. I want to be more than a nightlight to fall asleep in front of, or sound effects to do your homework by.

I guess what I'm saying is we should just cool it for awhile.

(FLIRTATIOUSLY) But now, tomorrow there *is* that terrific new show I want you to watch. And next week I've got some great new cartoons. And the week after that I've got a new mini-series starting. And . . .

(SHRUGGING SHOULDERS) . . . Oh, well, you know what they say—the best part about breaking up is making up!

(CONTINUING) . . . And then, there's that hysterical new sitcom premiering at the end of the month. And you're gonna absolutely love my line-up for the new season. And. . . .

BLACKOUT

"A fire-breathing dragon just ate my
straight A report card? My parents are
NEVER going to believe this!"

The Report Card Repair Shop

CHARACTER: Boy or girl
SETTING: Report Card Repair Shop
PROPS: Free-standing counter
    Sign that says "REPORT CARD REPAIR SHOP"
    Report card
COSTUME: Ordinary clothing

(OUR STAR APPROACHES COUNTER OF SHOP, REPORT CARD IN HAND)

(TO IMAGINARY CLERK) Uh . . . hi. I was just wondering if you could help me. See, I've got a report card here that needs . . . well, it needs some rather extensive repairs. (SETS THE REPORT CARD DOWN ON THE COUNTER)

I don't know what it is, but lately it's been stalling a bit in the academics, and work habits have been running a little rough. And, while you're at it, it appears classroom behavior could use a major overhaul, too.

. . . You ask how long has it been in this condition? . . . Well, I just noticed it today when the teacher handed it to me.

. . . What's that? . . . Didn't any warning lights come on?

Well, yes, there were those missed assignments, and notes home to my parents, and my test scores have been on the fritz for weeks now. But I had no idea it was this serious! . . . So, tell me, can anything be done or will I need to be towed into the next grade by six tutors and a live-in math teacher?

. . . First I'll need to realign my responsibility, overhaul my attitude, and recharge my commitment? . . . Okay, but what's all this going to cost? My play time? My T.V. time? My—I shudder to think—*nap* time?

. . . Really? All it's going to cost me is a determination to succeed? . . . Well, what about a guarantee? . . . You say you carry the standard 12-year or 50,000 homework assignments plan?

Well . . . (THINKS FOR A MOMENT) that *does* sound pretty good. Go ahead. Sign me up for the works!

. . . But, hey, in the meantime, you wouldn't happen to have a "loaner" card I could take home to show my parents, would you? (FROWNS) . . . Didn't think so.

BLACKOUT

Once Upon a School Day Dreary

If you have ever read the poem "The Raven," by Edgar Allan Poe, then you know this isn't it.

CHARACTER:	Boy or girl
SETTING:	In front of principal's office
PROPS:	Sign on door that says, "PRINCIPAL'S OFFICE— ENTER AT YOUR OWN RISK"
	Two chairs
	Empty album jackets
	Trash can
COSTUME:	Ordinary clothing

(OUR STAR SITS AT DOOR, FORLORN, LOOKING TOWARD AUDIENCE, ALBUM JACKETS ON NEXT CHAIR.)

Once upon a school day dreary,
While I daydreamed, bored and weary,
'Bout the fun and carefree places
I would rather be instead—

"I liked it better when they just called it the Principal's Office."

While I nodded, nearly napping,
Suddenly there came a tapping,
As of the teacher gently rapping
With a ruler on my head.

"What's the answer, please?" she questioned.
"Give the one I'm looking for,
Or it's this grade for one term more!"

I couldn't say one word or twenty,
But was I in trouble plenty,
So I tried to fake an answer,
As I've done so oft before—

But this time I couldn't do it.
When I spoke, I knew I blew it,
For saying the "Wright Brothers"
Was a rock group, made her sore!

That is why I am here waiting,
My punishment anticipating.
I'll prob'ly have to write eight million
Sentences upon the board.

I'll have to promise to start working.
Do my lessons. No more shirking.
And as for Orville and for Wilbur?
(PICKS UP THE ALBUM COVERS)
I'll buy their records . . . (TOSSES COVERS
INTO TRASH) . . . Nevermore!

BLACKOUT

"Hello. This is Alexander Graham
Bell. I can't come to the phone right
now because it's only 1875, and the
telephone won't be invented until
1876. But if you care to hold. . . ."

At the Sound of the Beep

CHARACTER: Alexander Graham Bell
SETTING: His workshop
PROPS: Work table
             Various tools
             Telephone with a very, very
             long cord
COSTUME: 19th century suit

(ALEXANDER GRAHAM BELL IS AT HIS WORK TABLE, BEFORE HIM VARIOUS TOOLS OF THE ERA AND HIS NEW INVENTION, THE TELEPHONE. HE PLACES THE RECEIVER TO HIS EAR, DIALS, WAITS A FEW SECONDS, THEN LOOKS OUT TOWARD THE AUDIENCE.)

I can't believe it! I finally got a dial tone! I invented this telephone a week ago, and I've been trying to get through to Mr. Watson to tell him the good news. But, boy, can that guy talk!

(HE PACES A BIT AND THE TELEPHONE CORD WRAPS AROUND HIM ONE TIME. BUT HE DOESN'T REALLY NOTICE.) But just wait till he picks up his receiver and hears me say, "Mr. Watson, come here, I want you." Why, he'll tell me I'm brilliant! He'll tell me I'm a genius! He'll tell me (LISTENS INTO THE RECEIVER, THEN LOOKS UP, PUZZLED.) . . . to leave my message at the sound of the beep?! (TO AUDIENCE) The guy's got an answering machine already? Boy, he sure doesn't waste any time, does he?

(INTO PHONE) Uh . . . yes . . . this is a message for Mr. Watson from Alexander Graham Bell. I just wanted to . . . Hey! Wait a minute! That couldn't have been thirty seconds!

(FRUSTRATED AT BEING CUT OFF, HE HANGS UP, PACES A FEW STEPS SO THE CORD WRAPS AROUND HIM AGAIN, THEN HE REDIALS THE NUMBER. AFTER A MOMENT, HE SMILES.) Ah, finally, a live person to talk to! (INTO PHONE) Hello, is this Mr. Watson? It's not? Well, then, who exactly is this? Really? Well, say, since I've got you on the line, I'll take a large pepperoni and sausage pizza and a two-liter bottle of root beer. Deliver it to the Bell's residence. You can't miss it. It's the only house on the block with a telephone pole in the driveway. (HE HANGS UP, REDIALS THE NUMBER, AND PACES AGAIN. ALL THE WHILE THE CORD IS GETTING WRAPPED AROUND HIM EVEN MORE. STILL, HE DOESN'T NOTICE.)

(INTO PHONE) Hello? Mr. Watson? *Again*, this isn't Mr. Watson?! Well, then, *who* have I gotten *this* time? . . . You say you're the operator and you want me to deposit ten cents for the first three minutes? . . . Listen, sister, this is *my* invention, and if I don't want to deposit ten cents, I don't . . . Hello? Hello? (INSULTED THAT HE'S BEEN DISCONNECTED, HE HANGS UP THE PHONE IN A HUFF.)

All right, Mr. Watson, this is it! I'm giving you just one more chance! (HE DIALS THE NUMBER, PACES, AND GETS HIMSELF EVEN MORE ENTANGLED IN THE CORD. BY NOW, ONLY THE ARM HOLDING THE RECEIVER IS FREE.) I tell you, if I don't get through to you this time, I'm . . . I'm . . . (HE LOOKS DOWN AND SUDDENLY REALIZES HE'S TIED UP, AND HIS ATTEMPTS TO UNWIND HIMSELF ONLY PULL THE CORD TIGHTER. IN THE MIDST OF HIS DILEMMA, A FAMILIAR VOICE COMES THROUGH ON THE OTHER END OF THE TELEPHONE. HE REACTS.) Hello?

Mr. Watson? I don't believe it! It's *really* you! And now, at long last I get to say what I've been trying to say all along.

Mr. Watson . . . (HE STRUGGLES TO GET LOOSE.) Come here. (HE TRIES FREEING HIMSELF AGAIN, BUT IN VAIN.) I want you. (HE MAKES ONE MORE TURN TRYING TO LOOSE HIMSELF, BUT INSTEAD TIES UP HIS ONLY FREE ARM. PITIFULLY, HE MANEUVERS THE PHONE TO HIS MOUTH.) Oh, and do bring some wire cutters!

BLACKOUT

Index